03/2013
Ø

What If We Do
NOTHING?

FOOD SAFETY

Carol Ballard

Gareth Stevens
Publishing

Please visit our web site at: www.garethstevens.com.
For a free color catalog describing Gareth Stevens Publishing's list of high-quality books, call 1-800-542-2595 (USA)
or 1-800-387-3178 (Canada). Gareth Stevens Publishing's fax: 1-877-542-2596

Library of Congress Cataloging-in-Publication Data

Ballard, Carol.
    Food safety / by Carol Ballard.
       p. cm. – (What if we do nothing?)
    Includes bibliographical references and index.
    ISBN-10: 1-4339-1982-6   ISBN-13: 978-1-4339-1982-4 (lib. bdg.)
    1. Food–Safety measures–Juvenile literature. I. Title.
TX533.B25   2010
363.19'262–dc22   2008052284

This North American edition published in 2010 by Gareth Stevens Publishing under license from Arcturus Publishing Limited.
Gareth Stevens Publishing
A Weekly Reader® Company
1 Reader's Digest Road
Pleasantville, NY 10570-7000 USA

Copyright © 2009 Arcturus Publishing Limited
Produced by Arcturus Publishing Limited
26/27 Bickels Yard, 151-153 Bermondsey Street, London SE1 3HA

Series Concept: Alex Woolf
Editor: Alex Woolf
Designer: Phipps Design
Picture Researcher: Alex Woolf

Gareth Stevens Executive Managing Editor: Lisa M. Herrington
Gareth Stevens Editors: Jayne Keedle, Joann Jovinelly
Gareth Stevens Senior Designer: Keith Plechaty

Picture Credits: Arcturus Publishing: 24 (Stefan Chabluk), 25 (Phipps Design), 29 (Phipps Design); Corbis: Cover, bottom left (Fritz Hoffmann), 7 (Gideon Mendel), 8 (Envision), 14 (Lowell Georgia), 17 (Romeo Ranoco/Reuters); Cover, top right and 21 (Peter Turnley), 22 (Reuters), 36 (Fritz Hoffmann), 42 (How Hwee Young/epa), 45 (Aristide Economopoulos/*The Star Ledger*); Getty Images: 11 (Sean Gallup/Stringer), 18 (Robert Browman/Stringer), 27 (Pascal Pavan/AFP), 28 (Ralph Crane/Stringer/Time & Life Pictures), 30 (Samuel Aranda/Stringer/AFP); Science Photo Library: 12 (Dr. Gary Gaugler), 16 (Bill Barksdale/Agstockusa), 32 (Philippe Gontier/Eurelios), 35 (David Parker), 39 (Cordelia Molloy); Shutterstock: Cover background (Ivan Cholakov), 4 (iofoto), 40 (Alexey Stiop).

Cover pictures: Bottom left: Fried chicken parts are sorted for freezing and packing at a chicken processing plant in Shanghai, China. Top right: A young victim of a cholera epidemic in a refugee camp in the former Republic of Zaire, 1994. Background: Bacteria viewed under a microscope.

Every attempt has been made to clear copyright. Should there be any inadvertent omission, please apply to the publisher for rectification.

Printed in the United States

1 2 3 4 5 6 7 8 9 14 13 12 11 10 09

Contents

CHAPTER 1

Food and Health

It is 2025. A serious outbreak of food poisoning has broken out in New York City, and many people are ill. Hospital services are stretched to the limit. Many hospitals now have space to admit only the gravest cases, such as the elderly and very young children. Businesses and services are finding it difficult to operate normally as their staff fall ill. Some schools have closed to prevent the illness from spreading among students. Scientists have been trying to trace the source of the outbreak. Initial results suggest that it may be linked to foods sold by a popular international food chain. However, the source of the contamination is proving extremely difficult to isolate because so many foods travel long distances among producers, retailers, and consumers. Tracking exactly how and where the outbreak started is a long and painstaking task.

Is Our Food Safe?

When we buy food at a supermarket, sandwiches at a delicatessen, or a meal in a restaurant, we assume that food is safe for us to eat. It looks appetizing and tastes delicious, but might eating it make us feel ill? Most of the time, food is safe. We eat and enjoy food without any bad effects. However, if food is not produced, packaged, and stored under appropriate conditions, it can spoil and present a health hazard.

There are many potential problems with food that can affect our health. Processed food might contain harmful microorganisms, such

Most supermarkets offer a wide range of imported foods from around the world.

as bacteria, which are responsible for outbreaks of food poisoning. Or processed foods might contain chemicals that are unsafe to eat. Many people argue that some modern ways of growing food are potentially hazardous to human health. Another source of potential harm comes from the water that we use to wash and cook our food.

Harmful contaminants may have entered our food at any stage: during production on a farm, during processing at a factory, or during storage at a food outlet. Even in our homes, problems may arise if we do not follow guidelines for the safe handling, storage, and preparation of our food.

FOODBORNE ILLNESS

This table shows the number of cases of foodborne illness in 2007 in the United States, France, and Australia. It is possible that the actual number of cases is considerably higher than these figures, as people often do not report mild cases to a doctor. The figures vary greatly from one country to another because methods of reporting and recording are different in each country.

Country	Cases of foodborne illness	Cases as a percentage of the population	Hospitalizations	Deaths
Australia	5,400,000	27.00	18,000	120
France	750,000	0.01	113,000	400
USA	76,000,000	26.00	325,000	5,000

Source: Australia – www.ozfoodnet.org.au; France – www.invs.sante.fr/publications/2004/inf_origine_alimentaire/inf_origine_alimentaire.pdf; USA – www.who.int/mediacentre/factsheets/fs237/en

Developed World

In the developed world, food producers follow routine procedures to ensure that food is safe. Food regulation agencies set standards for producing, processing, storing, and selling food. Food inspectors check all types of premises along the food supply chain. Food labels, for example, must include information about sell-by and use-by dates, ingredients, nutrition, and country of origin. That helps consumers make informed choices about what they eat.

However, there is a problem: Food comes from all over the world, and some countries set lower standards for food safety than others.

Developing World

In developed countries, food is abundant. There are plenty of choices of what to eat. People living in the developed world have the freedom to consider how safe food might be before they eat it. In parts of the developing world, though, food is scarce. People are often so hungry that they must eat whatever food they can find just to survive. For those people, food safety is less of a concern than it is in the wealthier developed world.

An international body called the World Health Organization (WHO) monitors food-related diseases throughout the world. It tries to encourage better food standards in developing countries.

Safe for All?

Not all problems with food safety are related to the quality of the food itself. A food may be perfectly safe for one person but be potentially harmful for another.

Food Allergies

An allergy is an unusual sensitivity to a particular substance, which can cause a strong reaction in a person's body. Many people are allergic to one or more types of food. When someone eats a food to which he or she is allergic, his or her body's immune system reacts to it. The immune system is the body's defense against foreign invaders, such as infections and other diseases. However, in some people, certain foods can trigger a defensive response from the immune system. Allergic reactions vary from one person to another but often include tingling in the mouth and throat, vomiting and diarrhea, skin rashes, and itching.

Which Foods?

It is possible to be allergic to any type of food. Milk allergies, egg allergies, soybean allergies, wheat allergies, and peanut allergies are all common in children, though many outgrow their allergies as they mature. Adult allergies include foods such as shellfish, fish, tree nuts (almonds, walnuts, and Brazil nuts), soybeans, and peanuts.

Opposite: Children from the very poor, rural Lusikisiki district of South Africa eat a meal. Many people in the developing world are under-nourished because food is scarce. For them, food safety is less important. Their top priority is getting enough food to eat.

The foods shown here (milk, strawberries, eggs, shellfish, and peanuts) can trigger allergic reactions in some people.

Avoiding Foods

People with food allergies usually try to avoid the foods that make them ill. Food packaging carries information about the ingredients the food contains. Some foods, such as nut oils, are used in shampoos and other products. Just putting those products on the skin can trigger an allergic reaction.

Extreme Reactions

Anaphylaxis is a very rapid and severe allergic reaction. The throat swells,

PEANUT ALLERGY

Allergies to peanuts are becoming increasingly common. They can be extremely serious and lead to anaphylactic shock. Many schools ban foods containing peanuts to reduce the risk to students. Peanuts are not actually nuts. Nuts, such as almonds, walnuts, and Brazil nuts, grow on trees. Peanuts, however, grow on smaller plants that are related to peas and beans. A person who is allergic to peanuts may be able to eat tree nuts without any allergic reactions.

preventing normal breathing. The blood pressure may drop, leading to collapse and loss of consciousness. Without swift treatment, anaphylaxis can be life-threatening. People at risk of anaphylaxis often carry medication to use at the first sign of an allergic reaction.

Food and Other Medical Conditions

Other medical conditions can also make it unsafe for a person to eat certain foods. For example, people with celiac disease are sensitive to gluten. That protein substance is found in many foods, especially those made from wheat, rye, or barley flour, such as cereals, breads, and pasta. Eating those foods may cause inflammation of the bowel, so people with celiac disease are advised to maintain a gluten-free diet.

Many people who suffer from migraines often find their attacks follow a meal containing a particular food, such as chocolate or cheese. By avoiding those foods, they can reduce the chances of having an attack.

WHAT WOULD YOU DO?

You Are in Charge

As the government official in charge of setting the agenda at a WHO conference on international food safety, which topics do you think should be addressed first?

■ Increasing access to clean water worldwide

■ Educating farmers about safe food handling, storage, and preparation

■ Educating people about food hygiene

■ Setting international standards for food safety and procedures for food safety inspectors

Which would have the biggest impact on food safety worldwide?

CHAPTER 2

Animals and Our Food

It is 2025. Politicians and health-care providers around the world are anxious. The number of cases of variant Creutzfeldt-Jakob disease (vCJD) has increased alarmingly over the last few years. The first human vCJD cases appeared during the 1990s. The most recent cases have been traced to a supply of contaminated blood. That blood was given to people undergoing surgery and to those with hemophilia and other conditions that require blood transfusions. Experts fear that millions of people may already be infected and that many of them will develop the disease in the future. Medical experts describe the situation as a "ticking time bomb."

What Is vCJD?

vCJD is the human form of a cattle disease called bovine spongiform encephalopathy (BSE). BSE is also known as mad cow disease (MCD) and was first discovered in Britain in 1986. It is similar to scrapie, an infectious disease found in sheep and goats. Scientists are not certain where BSE first originated, but it spread rapidly among British cattle. One reason for that was the common British farming practice of feeding cattle bonemeal made from cattle tissue. If the tissue contained brain and spinal cord material from a BSE-infected cow, any cattle eating that bonemeal could also become infected.

Scientists have discovered that BSE and vCJD are caused by faulty proteins in the brain called prions. Prions are similar to normal brain proteins, but are defective in how they are folded. Those imperfect prions affect other brain proteins and turn them into defective prions. As the number of defective prions in the brain increases, its cells are

vCJD AROUND THE WORLD

This table shows all cases of vCJD reported worldwide up to 2009.

Country	Total number of cases
United Kingdom	165
France	23
Other EU Countries	15
Republic of Ireland	4
USA and Canada	4
Saudi Arabia	1
Japan	1

Source: www.cjd.ed.ac.uk/vcjdworld.htm

damaged. Eventually, holes appear in the brain, making it look like a sponge. That brain damage leads to a rapid deterioration of brain function.

What Are the Symptoms of vCJD?

Early symptoms of vCJD include depression and personality changes, hallucinations, memory problems, and poor coordination. Those symptoms progress rapidly and are quickly followed by dementia (the loss of mental processing ability, including memory loss), movement problems, and eventually coma. Death usually occurs within a year after the first appearance of symptoms. However, there is a time delay, sometimes lasting many years, between infection and the first appearance of symptoms. That means that a person may be unaware that he or she is infected.

This calf is part of a herd of 198 cattle in Dresden, Germany. A case of BSE was detected in one cow in the herd, so the whole herd will be slaughtered to prevent the disease from spreading.

How Do Individuals Become Infected?

People can become infected with vCJD by eating BSE-infected beef or beef products. Since the first appearance of BSE and vCJD, governments have introduced new farming regulations. Those include:

- A ban on bonemeal feed for cattle
- The removal of brain and spinal cord tissues from cattle carcasses before processing
- The exclusion of older animals from the human food chain — the younger the animal, the less time it will have had to develop the disease

Other actions included routine monitoring of cattle for the disease, and the killing of herds of cattle, even if just one case was discovered. Some governments banned beef imported from countries where outbreaks of BSE had occurred. Those measures have reduced the incidence of the disease in cattle and decreased the chances of humans contracting vCJD by eating beef.

Microorganisms and Agricultural Animals

Microorganisms, also known as microbes, are too small to see with the naked eye. They include bacteria, fungi, and viruses. Many are harmless, but some can cause serious illnesses in humans.

Microorganisms can infect farm animals such as poultry, cattle, sheep, and pigs. The farm animals may pick up an infection from other animals, from animal waste, or from contaminated farm equipment. Even if the animal itself shows no signs of illness, the microorganism can enter the food products of that animal, such as eggs, milk, and meat. Humans can then become infected when they eat the infected food.

In many cases, people experience an unpleasant bout of food poisoning and recover after a few days. In other cases, particularly among the very old or very young, and among pregnant women, those infections can be serious and even fatal.

Preventing Microorganisms in Food

Animal products can become infected by microorganisms on the farm or at a later stage in the food supply chain. Precautions need to be taken at all stages. Most farmers try hard to keep their animals infection-free. They follow strict dietary, hygiene, and animal welfare guidelines. They may also give their animals medicines to prevent infections.

After leaving the farm, animal products are kept cold, in a freezer or a refrigerator. They may also be preserved in other ways, such as salting, smoking, and drying. Each of those methods prevents the growth of microorganisms.

Killing Microorganisms

Microorganisms in animal products can be eliminated in various ways. One of the best known methods is pasteurization, named after

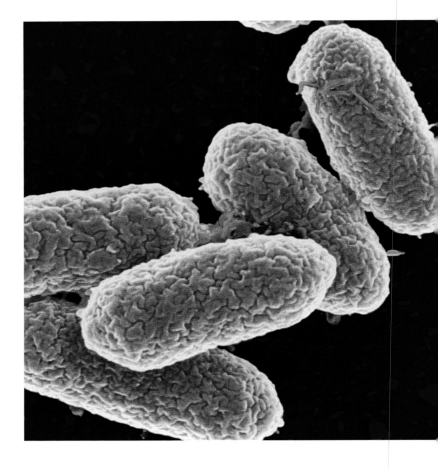

This photograph, taken using an electron microscope, shows a cluster of *Salmonella* bacteria. *Salmonella* is a major cause of food poisoning.

MICROORGANISMS IN FOOD

This table shows some of the bacteria that are found in foods from animals. Each bacterium causes sickness, diarrhea, and abdominal pains. People who get those symptoms after eating are sometimes said to have food poisoning.

Bacterium	Found in
Salmonella	unpasteurized milk, eggs, meat, and poultry
Escherichia coli (*E. coli*)	meat, unpasteurized milk
Clostridium perfringens	meat, poultry
Campylobacter	red meat, poultry, unpasteurized milk

the French scientist Louis Pasteur, who pioneered the technique in the 1860s. Pasteurization involves heating and then rapidly cooling liquids such as milk and juices to kill off harmful microorganisms.

Microorganisms can also be killed by irradiation — exposing food to radiation. Radiation is energy emitted in the form of rays or waves, such as X-rays, gamma rays, or beams of electrons. Each of those types of radiation is used to irradiate food.

Pasteurization and irradiation may reduce the nutritional value of food. Also, some scientists believe that irradiation may cause long-term health concerns due to the possible buildup of toxic chemicals in the food.

Cooking also kills microorganisms. It is important to ensure that fish, meat, and meat products are thoroughly cooked before they are eaten.

Other Animal Infections

Some microorganisms can infect farm animals but are not passed to humans via their meat or other food products. For example, the viruses that cause avian influenza in birds or foot-and-mouth disease in cattle cannot pass to humans via food products from infected animals.

Animal Medications

Farmers often give their animals antibiotics to prevent them from catching infectious diseases. Antibiotics are chemicals that attack bacteria. Alternatively, farmers might give their animals a vaccine. That contains a small amount of dead or weakened infectious material. The vaccine stimulates the animal's immune system to fight the infection should it encounter it in the future. Pests and parasites such as roundworms sometimes infect farm animals. Farmers can treat their animals with chemicals to prevent or control those infections.

The bigger an animal grows, the more food that can be obtained from it. Farmers sometimes dose their animals with growth

Technicians inject newly hatched chicks with a vaccine. This plant, in Maryland, produces chicks used in the broiler chicken industry.

hormones to increase their weight or to increase the quantity of milk produced by dairy cows.

While antibiotics, vaccines, pesticides, and growth hormones can help the farmer get the best return from his animals, they are not always beneficial for the consumer. Investigators have found traces of many of those chemicals in meat, dairy products, and produce. The chemicals can be harmful to humans. For example, the overuse of antibiotics by farmers can lead to the development of antibiotic-resistant microorganisms. Those cannot be killed by the usual drugs used to treat infections.

Animal Housing

Some animals are allowed to live much as they would in the wild, roaming freely in pasture. Some are confined to large, airy barns but still have space to move around. Others, though, are reared using intensive farming methods. They are kept in very confined spaces and have a strictly controlled diet. Some scientists suggest that food from intensively reared animals may actually not be as good for us as food from animals reared in more natural conditions. For example, a higher percentage of eggs from caged hens have been infected with *Salmonella* than eggs from free-range hens.

Environmental Pollution

Sometimes farm animals can be affected by pollution in the local environment. For example, wastewater from nearby factories may contain toxic chemicals that can soak into the soil and be taken up by plants growing there. When the plants are eaten by grazing animals, the chemicals enter the animals' bodies and are stored in their tissues. Researchers have found traces of those pollutants in some meats and meat products. When humans ingest that meat, they also absorb those pollutants.

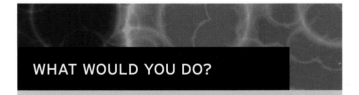

WHAT WOULD YOU DO?

You Are in Charge

As secretary of agriculture, which measures would you introduce in order to prevent a future outbreak of BSE or vCJD?

- Ask scientists to develop an effective screening test for cattle.
- Limit the age of animals entering the food chain.
- Ban the eating of beef and beef products.
- Ban the import of beef and beef products from countries known to have had BSE outbreaks.

What problems are you likely to encounter when trying to introduce any of the above measures?

CHAPTER 3

Plants and Our Food

It is 2025. Food safety inspectors recently found dangerous levels of pesticide residue on samples of both imported and homegrown fruits. Despite reassurances from farmers and retailers that the use of those pesticides has since ceased, the public remain unconvinced. Fruit sales have slumped to the lowest levels on record. Supermarkets have tried to entice customers back to the produce department with advertising campaigns and special offers, but have had little success. Many fruit farmers are facing economic ruin, and some have already gone out of business. Doctors are also fearful that people are no longer getting the vitamins and minerals they usually obtained from eating fresh fruit.

Herbicides, Pesticides, and Fungicides

Herbicides are chemicals that kill plants. Farmers spray crop fields with herbicides to kill weeds. Without weeds the crop plants do not need to compete for nutrients, water, and space. Without weeds in the fields, the crops can grow healthy and strong, with good yields. Weed-free crops are also much easier to harvest.

This airplane is spraying herbicide onto a soybean crop in Missouri to prevent weed growth.

Farmers also protect their crops from pests such as slugs, beetles, caterpillars, and aphids. They do that by spraying crops with a range of chemicals called pesticides. Some pesticides remain on the plants' surface and kill the pests when they come into contact with them. Other pesticides are taken up by the plants and kill the pests when they eat them. Fungi can also damage crops and may be controlled by the application of chemicals called fungicides.

Sometimes weeds and pests change, or mutate. Those mutations produce herbicide-resistant and pesticide-resistant strains. Existing herbicides and pesticides are ineffective against those new strains, so more powerful chemicals are needed to eliminate them. Farmers have few chemical-free options for effective treatment of those strains.

Fertilizers

To get the best possible yield from a crop, farmers need the plants to grow big and strong. To achieve that, they may use a range of chemicals called fertilizers. Those chemicals provide crop plants with extra nutrition and may be specifically formulated to suit the individual crop. However, chemicals from fertilizers can contaminate the soil and nearby water sources. They may also affect future crops or food sources such as animals raised on nearby land or fish in nearby rivers.

A mother gently comforts her 10-year-old son at a hospital in Bohol Province in the Philippines. A total of 27 children died after eating cassava (a kind of root vegetable). Doctors suspect they were poisoned by pesticides sprayed on the crops.

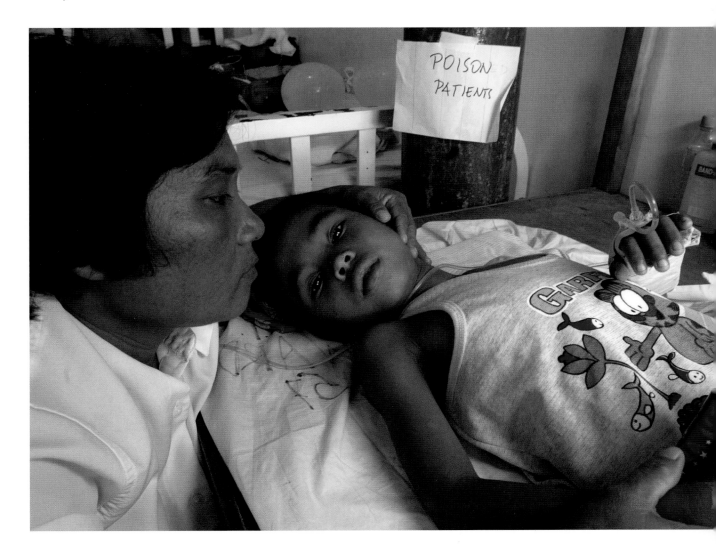

Scientists have found that some chemicals used to treat crops are harmful to human health. Some are also harmful to the environment and to wildlife. International and government organizations, such as the United States Department of Agriculture (USDA) and the European Food Safety Authority (EFSA), enforce strict rules that regulate:

■ The type of herbicides that can be used on crops
■ The concentrations at which those herbicides can be used
■ The frequency with which crops can be treated
■ The acceptable level of chemical residue allowable on food

However, some scientists, doctors, and environmental groups are concerned that chemicals currently considered to be safe may later turn out to be harmful. That was the case with dichloro-diphenyl-trichloroethane (DDT) and related chemicals DDE and DDD. Those

Workers inspect unripened tomatoes at a farm in Florida. Many tomato farms were inspected by the Food and Drug Administration (FDA) following an outbreak of *Salmonella* in 2008.

pesticides were once widely used on farms to control insects. The United States banned their use in 1972 after scientists recognized the environmental damage they caused. Later, scientists also discovered that they were harmful to humans, causing nervous system disorders, such as tremors and seizures. In women, those pesticides can increase the chances of having a premature baby. Despite that, DDT, DDE, and DDD are still used illegally in some countries that export food around the world, such as India and China.

In the case of legal herbicides and pesticides, food safety authorities set limits, called maximum recommended levels (MRLs), on the amounts that foods can contain. Scientists have found traces of chemicals from herbicides and other agricultural chemicals on many crops that exceed the MRL. Food experts advise people to wash all fruit and vegetables thoroughly before eating them or to cook them to remove traces of any remaining chemicals. Fruits and vegetables with skins that we remove before eating, such as oranges and bananas, will not have trace chemicals on their surfaces. However, they may still contain traces of herbicides and pesticides that the plant has absorbed.

Crop Infections

Crops can be infected by microorganisms such as *E. coli* and *Listeria monocytogenes*. Most crops are washed thoroughly before processing or packaging, but that will only remove surface microorganisms. Any microorganisms inside the plant will not be removed by washing. Infected fruits and vegetables can lead to outbreaks of food poisoning. An example of that occurred in the United States in 2008 when more than 1,400 people in 43 states became ill after eating tomatoes infected with *Salmonella*.

WHAT WOULD YOU DO?

You Are in Charge
As a health official, you are alarmed by the long-term health risks posed by reduced consumption of fruits and vegetables. How would you combat this?

- Subsidize fruits and vegetables so they are less expensive.
- Launch an advertising campaign informing people of the health benefits of eating fruits and vegetables.
- Launch an advertising campaign informing people about how tiny the risks are from trace chemicals.
- Make it compulsory for all children to eat fruits and vegetables as part of their school lunches.

Which of those measures do you think would be most effective?

CHAPTER 4

Water and Our Food

It is 2025. Many countries are experiencing a severe water shortage. Particularly badly hit are the countries of the Middle East, where rainfall has been much lower than normal. Many Middle Eastern cities have a high population density, poor living conditions, and a lack of sanitation. Together, those factors have resulted in a major outbreak of cholera in some poor urban districts. Medical workers are struggling to distribute antibiotics to the sick. To contain the outbreak, government officials are issuing emergency water purification tablets. Specially recruited sanitation officers are also disinfecting streets to prevent the disease from spreading. However, until there is sufficient water to allow people to maintain reasonable standards of personal hygiene, cholera will continue to be a serious health threat.

What Is Cholera?

Cholera is an intestinal infection caused by the *Vibrio cholerae* bacterium. It leads to sickness, vomiting, and diarrhea, which in turn lead to dehydration. If left untreated, cholera is usually fatal. Young children and the elderly are especially vulnerable to the infection. Cholera spreads when people come into contact with water contaminated with human feces. People can also catch the disease by eating food that was washed or cooked in contaminated water. In urban places where many people live in close contact with water and sewage that runs, spills, or leaks into water supplies, such as fresh rivers and lakes, there is always a risk of a cholera outbreak.

Treating and Preventing Cholera

Doctors treat cholera with antibiotics. Some vaccines have also been produced, but they are not widely available. People can reduce the risk of contracting cholera by maintaining high standards of sanitation and personal hygiene. That requires a good supply of clean water. In places where *Vibrio cholerae* is a risk, water can be boiled or treated with purification tablets for safe drinking.

Education

In developing countries, where water is scarce, people often have little choice but to use any water available to them. Governments, international organizations, and aid agencies are working to reduce the risk of cholera outbreaks. They are providing information about the dangers of contaminated water and educating people about how to properly boil and purify their water for safe drinking.

Cholera outbreaks frequently occur in situations where there is overcrowding and poor sanitation, such as in refugee camps. This Rwandan girl is the victim of a cholera epidemic at a refugee camp in the former Republic of Zaire.

JOHN SNOW AND THE BROAD STREET PUMP

In 1854, a cholera outbreak occurred In London. At that time, no one knew the cause of the disease. John Snow, a doctor, decided to investigate the cause. He thought the terrible living conditions of the poor and their lack of clean water might be responsible. Snow studied the pattern in which the infection spread and found it was centered on a water pump on Broad Street in the district of Soho. He removed the handle of the pump, preventing people from drawing water from it. As he'd expected, the infection stopped spreading. Snow became the first person to find a clear link between contaminated water and infectious disease. That was the beginning of the science of epidemiology — the study of the cause and transmission of diseases.

Typhoid Fever

Cholera is not the only waterborne infectious disease. Another example is typhoid fever, caused by the bacterium *Salmonella typhi*. Like cholera, typhoid fever is an intestinal infection that spreads via human feces. Outbreaks can also occur in overcrowded places with inadequate sanitation and a lack of clean water. Typhoid fever causes flu-like symptoms, which are followed by abdominal pain, diarrhea, and dehydration. Without antibiotic treatment, typhoid fever, like cholera, can be fatal.

Chemical Contamination

Even in developed countries, the water supply can become contaminated with harmful chemicals from factory and agricultural waste. At water treatment plants, dirty wastewater from houses, factories, hospitals, and other places that use water is collected. Here, the water goes through several different treatments to clean it and make it fit for human use. But the treatment plants cannot remove some medicines that might be contained in human urine, and those may contaminate the water supply.

BABY FORMULA

Mothers choose to either breast-feed their babies or feed them an artificial milk mixture called baby formula. Baby formula manufacturers have marketed their products to mothers in developing countries, telling them that their babies would benefit from formula. However, formula is a dry powder that must be mixed with water – a risky practice in countries where clean water is not readily available. Many babies have become sick after their mothers fed them baby formula mixed with contaminated water.

A man collects dead fish from a lake near Wuhan in Hubei Province, China. Wastewater from nearby factories has polluted Wuhan's lakes and rivers.

Industrial accidents sometimes lead to water contamination. In Camelford, United Kingdom, in 1988, 20 tons of aluminium sulphate were accidentally dumped into a tank at a water treatment plant. The chemical, which is used to remove cloudiness from water, was pumped to 20,000 homes in the North Cornwall area at very high concentrations. People exposed to the contaminated water reported a variety of health problems, and concerns remain about their long-term health.

Using contaminated water for washing or cooking food transfers any chemicals the water contains to those foods. The chemicals then enter our bodies when we eat the foods. Drinking water inspectors test water samples to ensure that they do not contain harmful microorganisms or exceed permitted levels of chemical contamination. Although individual countries set regulations and monitor water quality, most follow guidelines set out by the World Health Organization.

Chemicals in water can enter the food chain directly. For example, if chemical pollution from factories or farms enters rivers, the chemicals may be absorbed by fish and other aquatic organisms. If we then eat those fish, the chemicals enter our bodies.

WHAT WOULD YOU DO?

You Are in Charge

As secretary of health in a developing country with recurrent cholera outbreaks, which would you choose to spend your limited budget on?

- The purchase and distribution of antibiotics
- A construction program to improve sanitation and water supply
- The purchase and distribution of bottled water
- The purchase and distribution of water purification tablets

Which of those would provide the best long-term solution to eliminate or reduce cholera outbreaks in your country?

CHAPTER 5

Genetically Modified Food

It is 2025. People with peanut allergies are finding it increasingly difficult to be sure that the food they eat is safe. The media have reported several deaths of people with peanut allergies, even though they had not eaten any foods containing peanuts. The problem has arisen because scientists have created a strain of genetically modified (GM) wheat that contains genetic material from peanut plants. That genetic material gives an increased wheat yield, but it also means that people with peanut allergies are now also allergic to the wheat. A wide range of foods such as bread and pasta contain wheat. There is no way of telling which strain of wheat those foods contain. People with peanut allergies are now suffering the added restriction of being unable to eat any wheat-based foods, further reducing their food choices.

Genetic Modification

Every organism (living thing) contains a set of coded information called the genome, which is made up of units called genes. The genes, which exist in every cell of the organism, are carried by thread-like structures called chromosomes. Each gene is made from a molecule called deoxyribonucleic acid (DNA). The genes control every feature of the living thing. They are the means by which information is passed from one generation to the next. The chromosomes and genes they carry are known as the genome. Scientists have developed techniques for making changes to the genome. Producing those changes is called genetic engineering, or genetic modification.

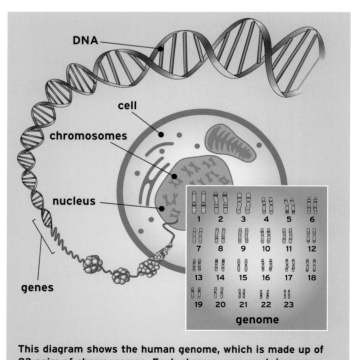

This diagram shows the human genome, which is made up of 23 pairs of chromosomes. Each chromosome contains many genes. Each gene is a particular section of DNA.

Selective Breeding

For thousands of years, farmers have selected the best of their animals or plants and used them to produce the next generation. Over time, that could result in an improvement in some characteristics of the animals or plants. For example, by breeding calves only from the cows that produce the most milk, a dairy farmer might expect the milk yield of his or her herd to increase a little with each new generation of animals.

Some varieties of crops are crossed with others to produce new plants that show the best characteristics of each. For instance, crossing a tall variety of bean that produces small pods with a shorter variety that produces a lot of pods could result in a tall, high-yielding variety.

GM Food

The genetic changes described above take place within a particular species. With genetic modification, however, scientists can transfer genetic material between organisms of different species. Critics of genetic modification say that process is unnatural. As we do not know all the dangers, they say, it should be banned. Supporters say it offers unlimited potential to increase and improve the world's food supply.

This graph shows how the production of genetically modified soybeans grew in major producing countries between 1997 and 2007.

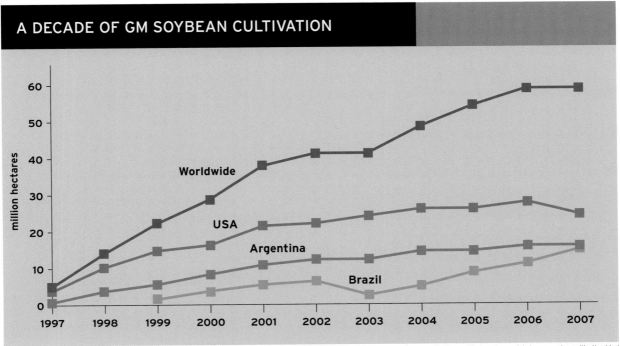

Source: www.gmo-compass.org/eng/agri_biotechnology/gmo_planting/342.genetically_modified_soybean_global_area_under_cultivation.html

Are GM Crops Good or Bad?

There is a lot of debate about the potential benefits and dangers of GM crops. Some of the main points on each side of the argument are given below:

Possible Benefits Cited by Supporters of GM Crops:

- Genetically modified crops can be developed to be resistant to pesticides and herbicides. That would allow whole fields to be sprayed, killing pests and weeds but not damaging the crops.
- GM crops can be resistant to pests, so the use of pesticides could be reduced.
- GM crops can be stress resistant. That would enable them to survive in conditions such as drought or extreme cold that would kill ordinary plants.
- GM crops that contain no allergens can be developed. For example, some GM peanut crops are being modified to remove allergens.
- GM crops can be developed with new characteristics to improve nutrition levels and increase yield to ease food shortages. Other GM varieties that contain vaccines and other medicines could also be developed.

Possible Dangers Cited by Critics of GM Crops:

- Genetically modified crops may damage native species. They may cross-fertilize with native plants, damaging them in ways from which they cannot recover. For example, GM-native hybrids may produce only sterile seed, which would not grow into new plants.
- GM crops may damage wildlife. They may have a negative effect on other plants and creatures by upsetting the balance of local food chains.
- GM crops may produce other harmful changes. The process of genetic modification may create unforeseen changes that could make GM crops harmful to humans.
- GM crops may cause allergy transfer. Swapping genes between organisms may also transfer the causes of serious allergies. People with allergies to particular foods would then also have to avoid other foods.
- Some GM crops produce only sterile seed. Farmers in developing countries often save seed from one season to plant the following year. If farmers are using GM varieties that produce only sterile seed, they would have to buy new seed every year. That could cause financial hardship for the farmers.

Different Views

Attitudes on GM crops vary around the world. In the United States, GM crops are grown openly on a commercial basis. In the United Kingdom, scientists are conducting field trials of GM crops. In other countries, such as France and Poland, GM crops are banned.

French activists destroy a field of GM crops. Those crops were part of a government-approved trial being carried out in Menville, France, in 2004.

WHAT WOULD YOU DO?

You Are in Charge

As secretary of health in a country where food shortages are a frequent problem, do you:

■ Encourage GM crops?

■ Ban GM crops?

■ Conduct field trials of GM crops for a period of time before deciding what to do?

Which of those courses of action would provide the food people need? Which would avoid any potential risks?

CHAPTER 6

Chemical Toxins and Additives

It is 2025. Doctors are concerned about the increasing number of patients showing signs of mercury poisoning. Mercury is a metallic element that builds up in the body over time and can cause damage to the brain and nervous system. Children are particularly at risk, as are babies before birth. Research has shown a direct link between the levels of mercury in patients' bodies and the amount of carnivorous marine fish, such as tuna, they have eaten. Tests on samples from those fish show they contain mercury levels much higher than most countries' food safety regulations permit. Tuna is now banned from school menus, and most people, especially pregnant women, avoid eating it. As a result, the tuna industry has collapsed. People who depended on tuna fishing, processing, and distribution have lost their jobs.

How Are Tuna Contaminated by Mercury?

Factories around the world dump industrial waste into rivers and seas. Some of that waste contains mercury. It is absorbed by tiny organisms called phytoplankton. Those organisms are eaten by small fish, which also absorb the mercury. The small fish are eaten by larger fish, which in turn are eaten by still larger fish, such as tuna. The mercury ends up in the tuna and eventually in humans who eat the tuna.

A food inspector is drilling into a yellowfin tuna to obtain a sample that he can analyze for its mercury content.

Concentrating Pollutants

The larger an organism, the more food it eats. The amount of mercury in a phytoplankton is very small. However, a single fish will consume many phytoplankton, and so the amount of mercury in that fish will be much greater by comparison. Similarly, a tuna must eat many fish. Therefore, the amount of mercury in the tuna will be many times greater than it was in the fish it ate. That increasing concentration of pollutants as they move up the food chain is called biomagnification. In some places, marine biologists have found tuna containing levels of mercury one million times greater than the amount found in the phytoplankton at the bottom of the food chain.

Mercury is not the only chemical that is found in carnivores at the top of the food chain. Others include lead, cadmium, some pesticides, and polychlorinated biphenyls from plastics. Biomagnification can occur with any pollutants that are absorbed by living organisms.

This diagram shows how a chemical gradually becomes more concentrated as it moves up the food chain. In this example, the chemicals are most concentrated in the larger animal, the hawk.

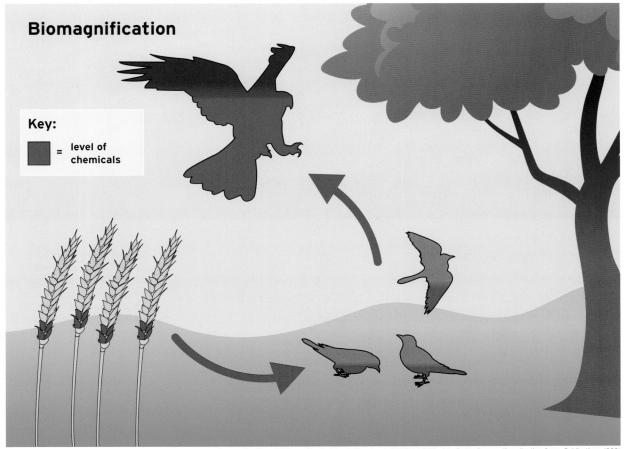

Biomagnification

Key:
= level of chemicals

Source: *Key Stage 3 Science: The Revision Guide – Levels 5-7* (Third Edition) by Paddy Gannon (Coordination Group Publications, 1999)

Chemicals From Air Pollution

Chemicals can also enter the food chain from air pollution. In many countries, air pollution is monitored and regulated to minimize the amount of harmful chemicals that are released into the air. In other countries, particularly those in the developing world, there is often little or no control of air pollution. Chemicals released from factories can pollute the nearby land and any food growing there.

Another source of air pollution is vehicle exhausts. Tests on foods, grown close to highways and other busy roads have shown high levels of harmful chemicals, including sulphates and lead.

Women work in a strawberry plantation in the shadow of a petrochemical plant in Palos de la Frontera, Huelva, Spain. Chemicals released from that factory may contaminate the crop.

Chemical Additives

Many chemicals are added to our foods intentionally. They are known as chemical additives, and they include:

- **Colorings.** Those make the food look more attractive. Many are harmless, but some have been linked to childhood behavioral problems. Some common colorings are tartrazine (yellow, E102, or FD&C Yellow 5) and Ponceau (red).

- **Flavor Enhancers.** Those improve the taste of food. A common flavor enhancer is monosodium glutamate (MSG). Some studies have linked MSG to brain disorders.

- **Preservatives.** Those help the food remain fresh. They give it a longer shelf life in a market and allow us to keep it at home for longer periods before we eat it. Sulfur dioxide, used as a preservative in foods such as dried apricots, is an additive known to aggravate asthma.

- **Emulsifiers.** Those prevent ingredients such as oils and water from separating. They are important in foods such as mayonnaises, margarines, and ice cream. Lecithin is a common emulsifier and may help to maintain a healthy circulatory system.

- **Gelling Agents.** Those make food more solid and less watery. Pectin is a gelling agent used in many jams and jellies. Pectin, which is found naturally in many fresh fruits, may also help reduce cholesterol levels in the body.

- **Vitamins and Minerals.** Those make the food more nutritious. Breakfast cereals often contain added vitamins and minerals. In some countries, folic acid is added to the flour from which bread is made. Adding vitamins and minerals to foods can help people who may not otherwise get enough of those nutrients in their regular diet.

ORGANIC FARMING

As we read in Chapter 3, pesticides, herbicides, and fertilizers play a significant role in intensive farming. Those products contain chemicals that can enter the food chain. Because of the unwanted effects that agricultural chemicals can have on humans and the environment, some farmers refuse to use them. Farming without chemicals is called organic farming. Critics of organic farming say that it yields less food per unit of land than nonorganic farming. At the same time, organic farming is more costly, so the prices of organic foods are higher. Supporters of organic farming say that lower yields and higher prices are costs worth paying to avoid the damage caused by agricultural chemicals.

Controlling Chemical Additives

In developed countries, regulations control which chemicals may be added to foods. Standards differ from country to country, so a chemical banned in one country may be permitted in another. For example, E107 (Yellow 7G) is banned in many countries, including the United States and Australia, but permitted in the United Kingdom. Imported foods and their ingredients are tested before they are allowed to enter a country to make sure they meet that country's standards.

Testing the Safety of Chemical Additives

Before a chemical is allowed for food use, scientists conduct a range of tests to make sure it is not harmful to human health. However,

A researcher tastes naturally occurring chemicals from food. She compares the taste of each chemical to that of the original food to see whether the chemical contributes to the flavor. If it does, it may be made into an artificial flavor to be added to food.

some health-care officials are concerned that current tests may not identify all the dangers associated with chemical additives. Some believe common chemical additives may be more harmful.

Food manufacturers must put labels on their products indicating the nutrients the food contains and a full list of its ingredients. That allows consumers to evaluate their food choices before eating.

When Things Go Wrong

Despite careful regulations and controls, mistakes can occur. For example, in 2005 there was a worldwide scare caused by a chemical called Sudan Red. That is a dye used in making oils, waxes, and polishes. It is not permitted in foods because it has been linked to an increased risk of cancer. However, during routine testing of a sample of chili powder, Sudan Red was detected. Around the world, food standards agencies, manufacturers, and retailers acted swiftly to withdraw the chili powder and any foods containing it from being sold.

Chemical Sabotage

Occasionally, individuals or groups have intentionally contaminated food with harmful chemicals. Such people usually act because they are angry at a particular manufacturer or retailer, or because they wish to make a political statement. For example, in 2002 a food retailer near Nanjing, China, used rat poison to contaminate food sold by a competitor. More than 200 people were hospitalized, and nearly 40 died. Authorities usually act swiftly to protect the public by ordering the removal of contaminated items from store shelves.

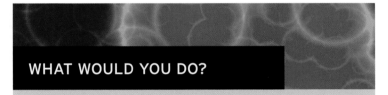

WHAT WOULD YOU DO?

You Are in Charge
As an official with responsibility for food safety, which action do you take first when you are told that a banned chemical additive has been found in a batch of food?

■ Alert the public via television, radio, newspapers, and the Internet.

■ Order the withdrawal of all affected foods from being sold.

■ Order an investigation to discover exactly how and from where the chemical was obtained.

■ Assess the risk posed by the additive before deciding whether to withdraw the product and alert the public.

Which would be the most effective way of protecting the public from the health risks associated with the banned chemical additive?

CHAPTER 7

From Producer to Consumer

It is 2025. Alarm is spreading as doctors detect the widespread presence of high levels of bisphenol A (BPA) in blood samples. BPA is known to be carcinogenic, which means it can cause cancer. It can also cause infertility and birth defects. BPA is used in food packaging, such as in plastic bottles. It is also used to coat the inside of food cans. Scientists believe that BPA has spread from the packaging into food and beverage products and then enters people's bodies when they eat or drink those products. Concerns about the safety of BPA in food were raised during the 1970s but were dismissed. Doctors do not yet know the extent of the problem, but because BPA is present in many food and drink containers, they are concerned that many people may be affected.

Chemicals and Food Packaging

Food is stored in a variety of containers from the time it is first produced until the moment we eat it. For example, as milk is processed, it passes from the cows' bodies, through pipes, and into

PLASTICS IN FOOD PACKAGING

This table shows some types of plastics and how they are used in common food packaging.

Name of Plastic	Abbreviation	Examples of Uses
Polyvinyl Chloride	PVC	Juice and water bottles
High-Density Polythene	HDPE	Milk bottles
Low-Density Polythene	LDPE	Yogurt containers
Polystyrene	PS	Frozen foods
Polypropylene	PP	Snack packets, squeeze bottles
Polypropylene Terephthalate	PET	Microwave meals, carbonated soft drink bottles

Source: www.bbc.co.uk/schools/gcsebitesize/design/foodtech/packaginglabellingrev2.shtml

storage containers. It is transferred into tankers and then travels through further processing stages. Eventually, the milk is poured into bottles or cartons to be sold. Every material and container with which the milk comes into contact must be safe.

Scientists test all new materials that will come into contact with food before permitting their use. They must show that the materials will have no ill effects on human health.

Since the first plastics were developed in the 1950s, increasingly complex materials have been used as food packaging. Most pose no risk, but some have since been found to be unsafe.

Plastic Wraps and Aluminum Foils

Some plastic wraps are coated with phthalates, or plasticizers, chemical materials that increase the flexibility of plastic. While those were safe to use on cold food, they became unstable when heated in a microwave oven. During the temperature change, chemicals were transferred from the plastic wrap into the food. New plasticizer-free wraps have since been developed, and those are thought to be safe.

This researcher is testing the safety of some food packaging. Her experiment will show whether chemicals are transferred from the packaging to the food when it is heated in a microwave oven.

Foils used for food packaging contain aluminium. Many people wrap food in foil before cooking it. That is safe with most foods but may be a risk with acidic foods such as fish with lemon or meat with tomatoes. That is because the acid in the lemon or tomato juices can react with the foil and release aluminium into the food.

Many foods are transported over long distances and undergo several processing stages between the farm and the consumer. At every stage, care must be taken to maintain the safety of the food. In developed countries, inspectors carry out regular checks on food producers, processors, transporters, and retailers to ensure that they meet strict food safety standards.

Workers at a food processing plant in Shanghai, China, sort fried chicken parts for freezing and packing. In order to maintain high standards of hygiene, workers must wear protective clothing.

SALMONELLA AT A PROCESSING PLANT

Twelve times in 2007 and 2008, the U.S. Food and Drug Administration (FDA) found strains of *Salmonella* at the Peanut Corporation of America's processing plant in Blakely, Georgia. Peanut products made by the plant caused outbreaks of *Salmonella* that sickened 502 people in 43 states and Canada. More than 300 of the plant's products were recalled. Even so, FDA inspectors reported finding *Salmonella* at the plant in January 2009. The FDA found that the company had tested its products, found traces of *Salmonella*, then conducted additional tests until it got more favorable results. It also failed to properly clean its facilities after the *Salmonella* bacteria had been discovered.

Processing

Many prepared meals contain foods that are made in large processing plants. Those plants must maintain good standards of hygiene and follow guidelines and regulations about safe food handling and storage. For example, staff working in those plants must wear protective clothing such as hats, gloves, and overalls to ensure that no contaminants pass from them into the foods they handle.

Transportation

Food must be transported safely from producer to consumer. Certain foods require special conditions. Foods such as soft fruits, milk, meat, and fish must be transported in refrigerated vehicles to maintain their freshness. Many foods are frozen before they are shipped. Eggs and other delicate foods may need special packaging to avoid damage during shipment.

Storage and Food Safety

There may be long delays between the production and the consumption of food. Throughout that period, food must be stored at the correct temperature. For example, chilled and frozen foods must be stored in refrigerators and freezers.

FOOD STORAGE METHODS

Method	How It Prevents Microorganism Contamination of Food	Examples of Foods That May be Stored in This Way
Drying	Microorganisms cannot grow without moisture	Beans, rice, pasta
Pickling and Salting	Microorganisms cannot grow in acid or salt	Vegetables, fish
Freezing	Microorganisms cannot grow in cold conditions	Premade meals, meats, vegetables
Vacuum Packaging	Provides a sterile barrier around food	Meats, cheeses
Canning and Bottling	Provides a sterile barrier around food	Fruits, vegetables
Modified Atmosphere Packaging (MAP)	Kills bacteria	Fresh salad greens

Traditionally, food is stored between harvest and consumption by methods such as drying, pickling and salting, and freezing. Each of those methods prevents the growth of microorganisms. Since the 1850s, scientists have developed techniques to ensure that the food we buy is safe to eat.

Pasteurization

Pasteurization is particularly useful for preserving dairy products, such as milk. Pasteurization is so widespread in most countries, such as the United States, that unpasteurized milk is rarely available.

Irradiation

Food irradiation is useful for preserving many types of food, including strawberries, raspberries, and other soft fruits. It is permitted in some countries, including the United States and parts of Europe. Other countries, such as the United Kingdom and Australia, have concerns about potential risks to human health, and its use is restricted to a limited range of foods.

Vacuum Packaging

Foods can be vacuum packed, which means that all the air is sucked out of the packaging. The package is then sealed so that no air can get back inside it. That process reduces food spoilage, keeping the food fresh for longer periods.

Modified Atmosphere Packaging

Modified atmosphere packaging (MAP) is a process of altering the internal atmosphere of a package in order to extend the shelf life of food. MAP is often applied to plastic bags containing fresh salad greens. The atmosphere inside the bags is changed so that it contains less oxygen and more carbon dioxide. Carbon dioxide kills bacteria, so modifying the atmosphere inside the bag helps keep food fresh.

New Packaging Materials

Scientists have recently developed "smart" packaging materials. Those are coated with a layer of nanoparticles (microscopic manufactured particles) that can detect chemicals inside the packaging, such as gases given off by microorganisms. Some packaging materials change color to indicate the food is not fit to eat. Others can kill microorganisms, keeping the food safe. Although smart packaging has potential benefits to increase food safety, some people think that more tests are needed to prove that it poses no risk to human health.

The strawberries on the left were irradiated with gamma rays after picking. The ones on the right were not. Several days later, the irradiated strawberries are still fresh, but the untreated strawberries are moldy.

Once food has been sold, responsibility for its safety passes to the person who buys it. Consumers should store, prepare, and cook food in ways that don't allow it to become contaminated. The best way to do this is to follow the "Four C" rule:

1. Clean

Wash your hands before you touch foods, and avoid coughing or sneezing close to food. Avoid preparing food for others if you have any symptoms of a foodborne illness such as nausea or diarrhea. Make sure the kitchen and all food preparation surfaces, such as chopping boards, are clean. All utensils, such as knives, whisks, mixers, and bowls, must be clean too. Keep the workspace free of clutter by disposing of packaging, peelings, and other unnecessary items.

2. Cook

Make sure all food is cooked thoroughly. Undercooked food can contain microorganisms that can multiply inside the body after the food is eaten, causing food poisoning. That is a particular risk when ingesting undercooked meats and meat products. Inserting a skewer into a piece of meat is a good way to check whether it is thoroughly cooked. If blood runs out of the meat, it needs more cooking time. Although some people like to eat their meat pink or rare, it is safer to cook it thoroughly. A range of thermometers is available for testing the temperature of foods. Some show only the temperature when you stick them into the food, while others indicate that the food is fully cooked.

This thermometer measures the temperature of the inside of the meat. From this information, the cook knows whether it is ready to eat.

3. Chill

Any fresh food should be kept chilled until eaten. That includes any leftover cooked foods, which should not be allowed to stand and cool at room temperature. Instead, they should be put into a refrigerator to cool.

4. Avoid Cross-Contamination

Use different chopping boards and utensils for each type of food. Colored sets can help to make sure you do this. For example, you could keep a green chopping board for preparing fruits and vegetables, a red one for fresh meats, a yellow one for dairy products such as cheese, and a blue one for frozen items. Use different utensils for cooked and uncooked meat. Different foods should also be kept apart during storage. For example, fresh and cooked meats should always be put on separate plates, wrapped separately, and kept apart in the refrigerator.

WHAT WOULD YOU DO?

You Are in Charge

As a government official, you have been given the task of increasing public awareness of food safety and hygiene issues. Which measure would you prioritize?

- Placing leaflets in doctors' offices, health centers, and hospitals
- Advertising on television, radio, newspapers, and the Internet
- Adding the topic to the school curriculum
- Starting after-school clubs for parents and children to learn about food safety

Which of those measures, do you think, would reach the most people and encourage them to follow the guidelines?

CHAPTER 8

Reducing the Risks

It is 2025. A food processing plant in a rice-growing country has broken international food safety standards. Scientists have found that some rice products made at the factory contain high levels of contamination with a banned chemical. However, the country's government refuses to recognize the international standards. The company running the plant insists its rice is safe and meets the country's own food safety standards. Many countries have reacted by banning the import of rice and rice products from that country. Food safety experts are worried about potential health problems. Governments are seeking ways to avoid a major international incident.

International Food Safety Standards

International food safety standards are regulations set up to ensure the safety of food worldwide. That is becoming an increasingly important issue as more and more food is transported around the globe. Several international organizations are involved, including:

■ World Health Organization (WHO), which published a Global Strategy for Food Safety in 2002 and set up the International Food Safety Authorities Network (INFOSAN) to improve international communications about food safety issues.
■ Food and Agricultural Organization (FAO) of the United Nations, which is involved in promoting food safety around the world.
■ European Food Safety Authority (EFSA), which oversees food safety issues within the European Union.

Most countries have their own internal food safety standards. In most cases, those are in line with international standards. Some countries, however, exercise few food safety standards, and those standards that do exist often do not meet international guidelines. That makes it difficult for those countries to export food to other countries.

A food safety inspector checks eggs imported from Malaysia before allowing them to enter Singapore.

Working to Improve Global Food Safety

A key role of the World Health Organization (WHO) is to help individual countries improve their food safety systems. The WHO sets international standards for the content and quality of food. It focuses on those stages in the food production chain "from farm to fork" where contamination of food is most likely to occur. The WHO provides information and guidance to countries on many topics, including:

- Foodborne disease outbreaks and incidents of food contamination
- How to improve the surveillance, identifcation, and isolation of foodborne disease outbreaks
- How to contain the spread of antibiotic-resistant microorganisms from animals to humans
- The safety of new types of food, including GM foods
- The safe handling and preperation of food

FOOD SAFETY REGULATORS

The following organizations regulate food safety in the United States:

Organization	Concerned With
Food and Drug Administration (FDA)	■ Protecting public health by checking the safety and effectiveness of food and drugs ■ Advancing public health by helping to speed innovations that make food and medicines more effective, safer, and more affordable ■ Helping the public get accurate information they need to use medicines and food to improve their health
Centers for Disease Control and Prevention (CDC)	■ Offering expertise, information, and tools to help people protect their health through health promotion, prevention of disease, and preparedness for new health threats
U.S. Department of Agriculture (USDA)	■ Food, agriculture, natural resources, and related issues
Environmental Protection Agency (EPA)	■ Environmental science, research, education, and assessment to protect human health and the environment

Inspecting Foods

Food hygiene inspectors visit every type of premises involved in the food chain, including farms, factories, slaughterhouses, shops, restaurants, and school kitchens. They check to ensure that adequate hygiene standards are being maintained and that the food produced is safe to eat and will not give rise to any illnesses.

ISSUES A FOOD INSPECTOR MUST CONSIDER

Topic	Issues to be Considered
Management	Are the managers aware of any hazards in their business? Have they set up systems to ensure the hazards do not result in contamination of food? Do they monitor all aspects of the business, and do they keep records to prove it?
Staff Training	Are all staff properly trained for the jobs they do? Are they all aware of their own responsibilities?
Temperature Control	Are temperatures of refrigerators and freezers checked regularly and recorded? Are cooked foods such as meat tested to ensure they are thoroughly cooked?
Cleanliness	Are all surfaces and equipment thoroughly cleaned?
Cross-Contamination	Are raw and cooked foods prepared and stored separately?
Staff Hygiene	Do staff have facilities for regular hand washing? Do they maintain high standards of personal hygiene? Are they provided with appropriate protective clothing?
Pests	Is there any evidence of pests on the premises?

After Inspection

The food hygiene inspector prepares a written report from notes taken during the inspection. A copy is given to the owner or manager of the premises, and another is sent to the appropriate authority. If the inspector is satisfied, no further action is necessary. If there are areas that need improvement, the report will contain recommendations and a follow-up inspection will take place to ensure they have been implemented. If the inspector believes the place poses a potential threat to public health, he or she can order its immediate closure.

Health inspectors check the kitchen of a restaurant in New Jersey to make sure that hygiene standards are being maintained.

What Can You Do?

Individuals can contribute to the safety of the foods they and others eat. Following guidelines for maintaining food hygiene when storing, preparing, and cooking food is important. People can also improve food standards in their community. For example, you could point out to a supermarket that you have noticed foods on their shelves with expired sell-by dates, or report unsanitary conditions in a shop or restaurant to the appropriate local authorities.

WHAT WOULD YOU DO?

You Are in Charge
As a WHO official, it is your job to decide the order in which global standards for food safety will be implemented. The options are:

■ farming

■ processing

■ packaging

■ public food outlets

Which of the above, do you think, has the greatest impact on food safety?

Glossary

additive A substance added to food

allergy An unusual sensitivity to a particular substance

anaphylaxis A very rapid and severe allergic reaction

antibiotic A medicine that can kill bacteria in the body

antioxidant A chemical added to foods to prevent deterioration

bacterium A type of microorganism that can cause infections

biomagnification The increasing concentration of a pollutant through the food chain

cell One of the tiny building blocks from which all living things are made

characteristic A distinctive feature of something

chromosome One of the thread-like structures that carry genetic information

contaminate Mix with something and spoil it

DDT A pesticide that was once widely used but is now banned in most countries

deoxyribonucleic acid (DNA) A molecule found in chromosomes that carries genetic information

emulsifier A chemical added to food to prevent ingredients from separating

fertilizer A chemical added to plants to promote growth

fungal To do with fungi

fungicide A chemical used to kill fungi

fungus A type of microorganism

gelling agent A substance added to food to make it less watery

gene An individual unit of a genome

genetic code The set of information that controls everything about an organism

genetic engineering A technique used to alter the genome of an organism

genetic modification Using genetic engineering to alter a genome

genome The complete genetic code of an organism

herbicide A chemical used to kill weeds

hormone A biological chemical that affects body functions such as growth

immune system The body's defense system

leach The absorbtion of material from one item to another

mercury A metallic element that can be harmful to the brain and nervous system

microorganism A living organism that is too small to be seen with the naked eye

nanoparticles Microscopic particles that have been produced to detect chemicals inside food packaging

nutrient Any of the substances in our food that our bodies can use

nutrition The nutrients in food

organic Grown without artificial chemicals

pasteurization The use of heat to kill microorganisms in food

pesticide A chemical used to kill pests

preservative A substance added to food to prevent it from going bad

prion Faulty proteins in the brain that are folded improperly

resistant Not affected by something

sterile Free from microorganisms

toxic Poisonous

toxin A poisonous chemical

vaccine A chemical that helps a human or animal fight a particular infection

viral To do with viruses

virus A type of microorganism

Further Information

Books

Ballard, Carol. *Global Questions: Is Our Food Safe?* (Franklin Watts, 2008)

Harmon, Daniel E. *What's In Your Food? Recipe for Disaster: Fish, Meat, and Poultry: Dangers in the Food Supply* (Rosen Publishing, 2008)

Sherrow, Victoria. *Point/Counterpoint: Food Safety* (Chelsea House, 2008)

Smith, Andrea. *In the News: Food Safety and Farming* (Franklin Watts, 2002)

Taylor-Butler, Christine. *True Books: Food Safety* (Children's Press, 2008)

Web Sites

Centers For Disease Control and Prevention (CDC)
www.cdc.gov
The CDC monitors and provides facts about disease outbreaks around the world, including foodborne illnesses.

U.N. Food and Agriculture Organization
www.fao.org
The Food and Agriculture Organization of the United Nations provides facts about a wide range of food supply and food safety issues around the world.

U.S. Department of Agriculture
www.usda.gov
This U.S. government organization oversees agriculture in the United States.

U.S. Food and Drug Administration
www.fda.gov
This U.S. government organization oversees all aspects of food safety in the United States.

What Would You Do?

Page 9:
Setting international food safety standards may be a beneficial long-term goal, but until every country agrees to implement and abide by them, food safety hazards will continue. Educating farmers about safe agricultural practices would help to increase food safety at its source, but educational programs should also include the people who process food. Educating people about food hygiene would eliminate some foodborne illnesses that arise in the home, but good food hygiene requires clean water and many people do not have access to that. Increasing the supply of clean water to all areas of the world is likely to have the greatest impact on food safety worldwide.

Page 15:
Banning the eating of beef and beef products would be impractical. It would provoke a public outcry and would be almost impossible to enforce. Banning the import of beef and beef products would have serious economic consequences and would generate anger from farmers, people in the meat industry, and other countries. Limiting the age of animals entering the food chain is a practical way of reducing the risk of future infections. Developing a screening test would identify any people already infected. Steps could then be taken to prevent victims from spreading the infection to others.

Page 19:
While students could be encouraged to eat fruits and vegetables as part of their lunches, making it compulsory is likely to be unpopular and unenforceable. People may react more positively to advertising that focuses on the health benefits of fruits and vegetables rather than advertising that draws attention to a health risk, however small that risk may be. Reducing the price of fruits and vegetables, with the help of government subsidies, is likely to encourage people to consume more. However, any tax increases needed to fund those subsidies might not be popular or possible.

Page 23:
The purchase and distribution of bottled water would be an appropriate response to an emergency situation but would not provide a long-term solution. Purchase and distribution of antibiotics would help people already infected, and water purification tablets would help people avoid future infections. However, provision of a reliable supply of clean water and a sanitation system for all is the only effective long-term solution to combat the disease.

Page 27:
Encouraging the planting of a high-yield GM crop might meet people's immediate food needs but could expose them and the environment to harmful long-term effects. Banning GM crops would remove any possible health risk from GM plants but would not solve food shortages. A balance between food shortages and possible risks from GM crops might be achieved by allowing some GM trials for a monitoring period, assessing the results, and then making a decision.

Page 33:
Ignoring a potential food risk, however small it may appear to be, is not a good idea, because it may result in some people getting sick. Ordering an investigation to find out what happened would be helpful but would not remove the immediate risk to the public. Alerting the public would help them avoid the foods involved. Withdrawing affected items from sale would also reduce the risk of anyone purchasing and consuming the contaminated foods.

Page 41:
Putting leaflets in doctors' offices, health centers, and hospitals would only reach people visiting those places. Although adding the food safety topics to the school curriculum and starting after-school clubs would reach children and their families, it would not reach people without children. An advertising campaign that covered a range of media such as television, radio, newspapers, and the Internet is most likely to reach and influence the majority of the population.

Page 45:
Implementing global food standards for public food outlets would have a positive effect in developed countries where people do eat out but would have little effect in developing countries where such outlets are rare. Implementing processing and packaging standards would only improve the safety of processed and packaged foods. The greatest effect on worldwide food safety may be achieved by implementing global food standards in farming and farming practices. That would affect all foods grown worldwide, regardless of any subsequent treatments they may receive.

Index

Page numbers in **bold** refer to illustrations and charts.

About the Author
Carol Ballard worked for many years as a school science coordinator. She is now a full-time writer of books for children and teens. Her books include *Fighting Infectious Diseases* (Watts, 2007).